MW01379617

Presented to:

Never Forget The Difference You've Made

Made in the USA
Columbia, SC
14 December 2022

73943992R00061